Before, After, and Always

Tiffany Williams-Parker

Presentation by *BookLeaf Publishing*

Web: www.bookleafpub.com

E-mail: info@bookleafpub.com

ISBN: 9789395756396

First edition 2022

DEDICATION

To William....dream big dreams.

Wicked Games

She sits on the steps,
like a damsel, waiting for distress.
With the sun in her face,
and the wind in her chest.
It's a similar story; the girl's a mess.
Tired of screaming, and trying her best.
Praying for peace, and finding nothing but
stress,
when coming to learn that the wicked don't rest.

Mama

"Mama," he calls me, and my heart is so full.
It's amazing how one word can light up my
world.
With his twinkling laugh, with his joyful grin
and his excitement for every place that he's been.
"Mama," he calls, and I'm always right there;
with a whisper, a laugh, or a hug we can share.
My greatest blessing and my biggest joy,
to see this world through the eyes of my boy.

Time and Space

There's a blank space in my memories
between who I am and what is meant for me.
A black spot of uncertainty, a longing for clarity,
a searching in the dark for what's meant to be.
Safety in numbers is meaningless here,
looking for answers in the underside of fear.
A spot of happiness rising from the mist
like a delicate flower held tight in my fist.
A journey through time like the slowest race,
biding my time until I find my place.

Siren Song

Love is like a siren song;
a wave of emotion pulling you into the deep.
A melody that leads you into all that makes you
human.
Venturing forward does not secure safe passage.
The waters are rough,
and the heart is hard to navigate.
So you cling to your life raft and pray not to
drown,
in the song, in the promise, in that most beautiful
sound.

As Time Flies

5

Time is a thief, and a fickle friend.
Slow to start, but quick to end.
Days turn to weeks, turn to memories past;
blink too soon and it's gone so fast.
Child to adult with a turn of the head;
sandbox to first dance to "I thee wed."
What would it take to hold onto that youthful
wonder?
Before the weight of responsibility pulls you
under?

Loving You

I love you.
I love you in all of the ways.
Like a bee loves flowers, or flowers love the
rain,
I love you.
With youthful wonder and butterflies in my
chest,
I love you. Even when I don't.
Even in the in between, and the upside down
spaces, where love runs away.
I love you, like a promise, like a choice.
I choose to love you. In all of the ways.

Rainfall

The night smells like the rain that never falls.
Smells of a cleansing, of a promise.
Like a prayer of renewal and reunion.
But the rain never falls.

Family Ties

What makes a family?
It is the people who make us, or the people we
choose?
I like to think it's a combination of both.
Because the people we choose, are the people
who make us.
The ones we love, shaping pieces of us as they
move through our lives.
Family breaks, and family binds.
So we hold tight to our chosen people,
as a way to guide us home.

New Beginnings

Hello there again,
so good to see you old friend.
Tell me everything that's new;
tell me the things to love about you.
Starting over, like a new day,
chasing all fear and doubt away.
Like an old song rewritten with new music and
lines,
new chords playing over memories of old times.
Take my hand and walk with me,
let's discover who we're meant to be.

The Love of a Child

Your first cry in this world was my first true
breath of life;
the moment I knew that my purpose was to
make your dreams come true.
The smallest soulmate, the biggest joy.
Loving you is like breathing;
all consuming and life saving.

Falling

Help me fly, don't let me fall.
Within my grasp, I can have it all.
My wildest dreams, laced with my deepest fears.
Ending and beginning, through all of my years.
Flying and flailing,
twisting in the wind.
Ready to jump, but scared to begin.
Making my way through time and through
space,
hoping for peace and praying for grace.

Belief in the Face of the Unknown

Breathe in slowly,
and let it out.
Take a step before you drown.
Close your eyes,
and count to ten.
Let your day begin again.
Say a prayer,
whisper,
shout.
Hold your dreams, push away your doubts.
Have faith in what you want from life;
have no regrets, stay in the fight.
Believe in what you know is true,
believe in what I say to you.

I Do

We close our eyes, take a breath and leap;
over the edge of a cliff that's too steep.
Into the future, where two souls meet as one;
hands clasped together, and faces turned to the
sun.
It's a beautiful future, the knife's edge of a
dream;
a life to be lived, adventures to be seen.
A house, a family, a child or two;
a life that is started with a breath and "I do."

Tell Me An Ending

Tell me an ending, a memory to last;
our story is fading and I'm losing our past.
Give me a minute, give me a sign;
a clue of how to move forward without wasting
my time.
Show me a path, light up a way through;
to a better beginning, to a new version of you.
Tell me an ending but make it loving and true;
so that we can write a new story of how we
started anew.

These Women

These women have grown weary,
wary,
wronged.
By a bleak and blackened world that hates that
we are strong.
It's that same strength that keeps us burning,
keeps us fighting,
keeps us brave.
Keeps us from succumbing to being dolls locked
in a cage.
These women have grown scary, but in the best
of ways;
in ways that bring reassurance that we will soon
see better days.

Dreaming

In the middle of the night, I dream my biggest dreams.
The ones that buzz like neon lights reflecting in the rain.
The dreams that are still there when I wake up,
That make me believe I can do anything and be anyone.
In the middle of the night, my biggest dreams come alive.
Dancing behind my eyes like a performer's opening night.
Spinning me around, and sending me leaping into the future.
In the middle of the night, my biggest dreams wake me.
Like the monster under the bed, a fear of the unknown cutting through and pushing me forward.
In the middle of the night, it's all a dream.

Secrets

Got a secret, you can't keep it, what lie do you
tell yourself?
Keep it quiet, keep it sacred, keep those thoughts
high on a shelf.
But in public, you are happy,
you are smiling, you're a prize.
Take a new path, write a new song,
try a new life on for size.
You have secrets,
they stay secret, they stay written on your heart.
You'll take them with you, through the ending,
you will never be apart.

Before, After and Always

Before, she was wild.
The brightest neon, buzzing in the wind.
Before, she was a frenzy;
spinning and whirling, like tomorrow would
never come.

After, she was quiet, but wiser.
A calm in a storm, a steady drumbeat coming
down the line.
After, she was braver;
a force of nature, a perfect heartbeat keeping
time.

Always…she was free.